THE NINE-FIGURE MENTALITY

MENTALITY

**A Guide to Achieving a Net Worth
Exceeding $100 million from Scratch**

Traci Fischer

CONTENTS

Chapter 1: Introduction

In a realm where financial aspirations often revolve around numerical magnitudes, the Nine-Figure Mindset emerges as a ground-breaking philosophy for wealth creation. It transcends the mere accumulation of riches, embodying a comprehensive set of principles, strategies, and mental frameworks that propel individuals toward unparalleled financial success.

Central to the Nine-Figure Mindset is the capacity to envision possibilities beyond traditional confines. It involves daring to dream on a scale not measured in millions but in hundreds of millions. Visionary thinking encompasses the ability to identify lucrative opportunities, anticipate market trends, and strategically shape the future rather than merely reacting to the present.

Attaining a nine-figure net worth necessitates meticulous planning and strategic decision-making. Those with the Nine-Figure Mindset approach financial endeavours with the precision of chess grandmasters, calculating moves with an eye on long-term implications. Each decision, whether in investments or business ventures, contributes as a vital piece to the larger wealth-building strategy.

The Nine-Figure Mindset champions the notion that calculated risks serve as catalysts for substantial rewards. It does not advocate reckless gambling; instead, it encourages navigating uncertainties with confidence, thorough research, and a willingness to venture beyond comfort zones. Risk is viewed not as a hindrance but as a strategic force propelling financial growth.

In a swiftly evolving landscape, stagnation impedes financial progress. The Nine-Figure Mindset thrives on perpetual innovation. Whether disrupting industries, introducing ground-breaking products, or pioneering novel investment strategies, adherents are at the forefront of change. Adaptability and an unwavering pursuit of improvement are integral aspects of their approach to wealth creation.

Beyond numerical metrics, the Nine-Figure Mindset underscores holistic success. It extends beyond the balance sheets and portfolios, encompassing positive contributions to society, fostering meaningful relationships, and maintaining a harmonious work-life balance. Adherents understand that genuine prosperity goes beyond financial metrics, emphasizing a comprehensive and fulfilling approach to success.

Essentially, the Nine-Figure Mindset signifies a paradigm shift—an encouragement to think expansively, strategize shrewdly, and pursue financial success with unparalleled determination. It challenges norms, redefines limitations, and sets the stage for a transformative journey from zero to a net worth exceeding $100 million.

Importance of a Growth Mindset in Wealth Building

The essence of a growth mindset becomes pivotal in the pursuit of prosperous wealth building, moving beyond mere monetary considerations to instil a mindset characterized by resilience, adaptability, and continual evolution. Recognizing the profound importance of this mindset in the context of financial success unveils a pathway to sustainable wealth creation.

They include:

1. Viewing Challenges as Learning Opportunities

A growth mindset perceives challenges not as insurmountable barriers but as chances for learning and improvement. In the domain of wealth building, encountering setbacks is inevitable. However, those with a growth mindset regard these challenges as stepping stones towards refining their strategies, gaining valuable experience, and ultimately enhancing their financial expertise.

2. Tenacity and Resilience in Wealth Endeavours

The journey of wealth building seldom follows a linear trajectory. It requires tenacity and resilience to navigate the inevitable peaks and valleys. A growth mindset instils the belief that sustained effort and dedication lead to mastery. Individuals embracing wealth creation with this mindset comprehend that setbacks are not enduring failures but temporary obstacles on the path to success.

3. Continuous Learning and Skill Enhancement

A growth mindset is marked by an insatiable thirst for knowledge and a commitment to ongoing learning. In the ever-changing landscape of finance, staying ahead necessitates perpetual adaptation. Those with a growth mindset actively seek opportunities to broaden their skill set, stay abreast of market trends, and adopt lifelong learning as a pivotal strategy for sustained wealth building.

4. Effective Risk Navigation

Wealth building entails calculated risks. A growth mindset facilitates adept risk management by encouraging individuals to assess risks, learn from outcomes, and adjust strategies accordingly. Rather than dreading failure, those with a growth mindset use it as a tool for refining their approach, optimizing decision-making processes, and ultimately mitigating future risks.

5. Fostering a Constructive Relationship with Success and Failure

Success and failure intertwine in the wealth-building journey. A growth mindset fosters a positive perspective on both outcomes. Success is perceived as a product of effort and effective strategies, while failure is reframed as a valuable learning opportunity. This mindset diminishes the fear of failure, empowering individuals to take calculated risks that can lead to significant financial gains.

6. Adapting to Market Dynamics

Financial markets are dynamic and subject to continual change. A growth mindset equips individuals with the flexibility and adaptability necessary to navigate these fluctuations. Instead of resisting change, those with a growth mindset embrace it as an opportunity to innovate, seize emerging trends, and position themselves strategically for sustained financial growth.

In essence, the importance of a growth mindset in wealth building transcends financial principles; it's a guiding philosophy that empowers individuals to see challenges as opportunities, persist in adversity, and approach wealth creation as a dynamic, lifelong journey of learning and growth.

Chapter 2: Foundation for Financial Success

Establishing a robust foundation is crucial for embarking on the journey toward financial success. This section delves into key elements that form the bedrock of prosperity, emphasizing the significance of setting clear goals, cultivating a positive money mindset, and developing strong financial habits.

Setting Clear Goals and Objectives

Establishing well-defined financial goals is comparable to mapping out a route for success in the expansive realm of wealth building. This involves not only envisioning the destination but also strategizing the specific path to reach it.

1. Distinguishing Short-Term and Long-Term Goals

Commence the goal-setting process by discerning between short-term and long-term financial objectives. Short-term goals provide immediate targets for a sense of accomplishment, while long-term goals lay out a plan for sustained wealth accumulation. This dual perspective enables a flexible and balanced approach to financial planning.

Example: Short-term goals could involve creating an emergency fund or paying off high-interest debt, while long-term goals may include achieving financial independence, acquiring a home, or funding a child's education.

2. Implementing SMART Goal Setting

Apply the SMART criteria to structure goals effectively. Ensuring that goals are Specific, Measurable, Achievable, Relevant, and Time-Bound provides a clear framework for action. This approach transforms aspirations into tangible targets, facilitating progress tracking and informed adjustments as needed.

Example: Instead of a broad goal like "save money," a SMART goal might be "Save $10,000 within the next 12 months by contributing $800 per month to an investment account."

3. Aligning Goals with Personal Values

Confirm that financial goals align with individual values and life priorities. This alignment infuses depth and meaning into the pursuit of wealth, turning it from a numerical exercise into a journey that resonates with core beliefs. It also boosts motivation by linking financial objectives with broader life aspirations.

Example: If family and experiences are valued, a goal could involve allocating a specific budget for annual family vacations.

4. Monitoring Progress and Celebrating Achievements

Regularly assess and track progress toward financial goals. Establishing milestones enables incremental celebrations of accomplishments, reinforcing dedication and motivation. This monitoring process also allows for adjustments to strategies as circumstances change.

Example: Celebrate reaching a savings milestone by rewarding yourself or acknowledging progress toward debt reduction with a sense of achievement.

5. Periodic Review and Adaptations

Recognize that goals and circumstances may evolve. Engage in periodic reviews to evaluate whether goals remain pertinent and attainable. Adjustments to the plan may be necessary based on changes in income, expenses, or external factors. This adaptability ensures that the financial plan remains responsive to individual needs and aspirations.

Example: If career advancements lead to increased income, consider adjusting savings goals or exploring new investment opportunities.

In essence, setting clear goals and objectives is not a rigid process; it's a dynamic and deliberate navigation of one's financial journey. Through intentional planning, alignment with personal values, and a commitment to flexibility, individuals can forge a path towards financial success with clarity and purpose.

Nurturing a Positive Money Mindset

The process of nurturing a positive money mindset entails a transformative journey that involves reshaping one's attitudes and beliefs about wealth, thereby influencing financial decisions and overall well-being.

1. Embracing an Abundance Mentality

Challenge a scarcity mindset by adopting an abundance mentality. Instead of perceiving resources and opportunities as limited, foster the belief that abundance surrounds you. This shift in perspective encourages proactive thinking, enabling a more optimistic approach to financial decision-making.

Example: Rather than fretting over financial constraints, focus on the array of growth opportunities, recognizing the diverse paths to prosperity.

2. Mindful Financial Decision-Making

Infuse mindfulness into financial choices. Being present and conscious of each financial decision prevents impulsive behaviours and encourages thoughtful spending. Mindfulness fosters an awareness of the present financial situation, promoting responsible decision-making and reducing unnecessary stress related to money.

Example: Before making a significant purchase, take a moment to reflect on its alignment with your financial goals and explore alternative, more cost-effective options.

3. Expressing Gratitude for Financial Well-being

Integrate gratitude into financial practices. Regularly acknowledge and appreciate current financial achievements, regardless of their scale. Expressing gratitude for what you have fosters contentment and satisfaction, reducing the inclination for unnecessary spending driven by a desire for more.

Example: Keep a gratitude journal where you document small financial victories or express appreciation for the financial stability you currently enjoy.

4. Positive Visualization and Affirmations

Engage in positive visualization and affirmations related to financial success. Envisioning a prosperous future and affirming positive beliefs about your financial capabilities can rewire your subconscious mind. This practice boosts confidence, enhances motivation, and attracts opportunities aligned with your financial goals.

Example: Dedicate a few minutes each day to visualize achieving your financial goals, complemented by affirmations such as "I possess the skills to create and manage wealth."

5. Learning from Setbacks with a Growth Mindset

Approach setbacks with a growth mindset. Instead of perceiving financial challenges as insurmountable obstacles, view them as opportunities for learning and improvement. Embracing the idea that failures are stepping stones to success fosters resilience and a proactive attitude toward overcoming financial hurdles.

Example: If an investment falls short of expected returns, analyse the situation, extract valuable lessons, and adjust your strategy for future investments.

6. Surrounding Yourself with Positive Influences

Surround yourself with positive influences that reinforce a healthy money mindset. Connect with individuals who share a similar financial philosophy, participate in seminars or workshops emphasizing positive financial habits, and consume content that inspires and motivates prudent financial behaviour.

Example: Joining a financial support group or engaging in online forums with a positive financial focus can provide encouragement and valuable insights.

In essence, nurturing a positive money mindset involves intentionally reshaping thoughts and beliefs surrounding wealth. By embracing an abundance mentality, practicing mindfulness, expressing gratitude, visualizing success, viewing setbacks as opportunities, and surrounding yourself with positivity, you can foster a mindset conducive to sustainable financial well-being.

Cultivating Robust Financial Practices

Nurturing robust financial habits is the cornerstone of enduring prosperity, guiding individuals toward responsible financial stewardship and prolonged wealth accumulation.

1. Effective Budgeting and Expense Monitoring

Implementing a thorough budgeting strategy forms the basis of financial discipline. Consistently monitor income and expenses to gain a transparent understanding of financial flows. This practice not only ensures well-informed decision-making but also encourages mindful spending.

Example: Utilize budgeting apps or tools to categorize expenditures, establish spending limits, and regularly assess financial progress.

2. Consistent Saving and Investment Practices

Foster a routine of regular saving and investing. Allocating a portion of income consistently not only establishes a financial safety net but also harnesses the benefits of compounding. This sustained approach facilitates wealth accumulation and provides a buffer against unforeseen financial challenges.

Example: Automate monthly transfers to a savings or investment account for consistent contributions.

3. Sound Debt Management Approaches

Developing sound debt management practices is crucial for financial stability. Prioritize debt repayment, avoid unnecessary debt accumulation, and employ responsible credit utilization. These habits contribute not only to maintaining a positive credit score but also free up resources for wealth-building pursuits.

Example: Develop a debt repayment plan by prioritizing high-interest debts and allocating additional funds for timely repayment.

4. Continuous Financial Learning

Ingrain a routine of continuous financial education to stay abreast of economic trends, investment opportunities, and personal finance strategies. Actively seek out resources, participate in workshops, and engage in ongoing learning endeavours to enhance financial literacy.

Example: Stay informed by subscribing to reputable financial publications, following industry blogs, and attending webinars.

5. Prioritizing Emergency Fund Establishment

Give precedence to establishing and growing an emergency fund. A robust financial habit involves setting aside funds to cover unforeseen expenses, offering a financial cushion during challenging times and mitigating the need to tap into long-term investments.

Example: Strive to save three to six months' worth of living expenses in an easily accessible emergency fund.

6. Prudent Consumer Practices

Cultivate prudent consumer practices by making well-informed purchasing decisions. Distinguish between needs and wants, compare prices, and seek value for money. This habit not only contributes to judicious financial management but also prevents undue financial strain.

Example: Conduct thorough research, compare prices across different retailers, and explore cost-effective alternatives before making a purchase.

7. Regular Setting and Review of Financial Goals

Integrate the practice of regularly setting and revisiting financial goals. This approach provides a sense of purpose, motivation, and a framework for decision-making, ensuring that financial efforts align with overarching objectives.

Example: Establish specific financial goals, such as saving for a home down payment or funding education, and periodically evaluate progress.

Cultivating robust financial practices is an ongoing journey that demands commitment and discipline. By incorporating budgeting, saving, informed consumer practices, and a dedication to financial education, individuals can establish a sturdy foundation for enduring financial success.

Chapter 3: From Zero to First Million

Embarking on the journey from zero to the first million requires a strategic approach, discipline, and a keen understanding of wealth-building principles. This section explores key strategies, including building a solid income stream, implementing strategic saving and investment practices, and leveraging opportunities for growth.

Establishing a Strong Income Stream

Laying the groundwork for a robust income stream is fundamental to achieving financial success, demanding strategic foresight, diversity, and proactive engagement in both career and entrepreneurial pursuits.

1. Deliberate Career Planning

Formulating a deliberate career plan involves aligning personal strengths and ambitions with market needs. Recognizing industries with high growth potential and acquiring sought-after skills provides the basis for a strong income stream. Ongoing professional development ensures adaptability in a dynamic job market.

Example: Regularly assess skills, stay abreast of industry trends, and pursue certifications or training programs to enhance professional appeal.

2. Venturing into Entrepreneurship

Exploring entrepreneurship serves as a potent method for broadening income sources. Initiating a side business or investing in scalable startups allows individuals to channel creativity and potentially generate passive income. Entrepreneurial pursuits can substantially contribute to wealth accumulation beyond traditional employment.

Example: Identify market gaps, develop a viable business plan, and gradually transition into entrepreneurship while maintaining a primary income source.

3. Strategic Salary Negotiation

Mastering strategic salary negotiation is pivotal for maximizing earnings. Thorough research on industry benchmarks, highlighting achievements, and negotiating compensation packages commensurate with one's value contribute to incremental salary growth over time.

Example: Before negotiations, compile data on industry salary standards, showcase key accomplishments, and articulate the unique value brought to the organization.

4. Investing in Education and Skill Enhancement

Investing in education and skill enhancement is an ongoing effort that elevates professional expertise. Continuous learning not only positions individuals for career advancement but also augments earning potential. Acquiring specialized skills opens doors to higher-paying opportunities.

Example: Enrol in pertinent courses, attend workshops, and engage in webinars to stay current on industry developments and maintain a competitive edge.

5. Diversification of Income Streams

Diversifying income streams guards against financial volatility and bolsters overall financial resilience. Exploring avenues such as investments, freelance work, or royalties from creative pursuits establishes multiple income channels, reducing dependence on a single source.

Example: Explore opportunities for freelance or contract work alongside a primary job, invest in dividend-paying stocks, or engage in passive income streams like real estate.

6. Strategic Networking and Professional Bonds

Building and nurturing a robust professional network is invaluable for uncovering fresh opportunities. Networking facilitates access to job prospects, potential partnerships, and insights into industry trends. Fostering professional relationships can lead to referrals, mentorship, and collaborative ventures.

Example: Attend industry events, participate in online professional communities, and actively connect with colleagues to expand and sustain a resilient professional network.

7. Exploration of Supplementary Income Activities

Beyond conventional employment, exploring supplementary income activities contributes to financial growth. Engaging in consulting, freelance work, or monetizing hobbies can supplement primary income and expedite progress toward financial objectives.

Example: Provide consulting services in areas of expertise, explore freelance opportunities in niche markets, or monetize creative talents through platforms like freelancing websites or online marketplaces.

Establishing a strong income stream demands a proactive and diversified strategy. Through deliberate career planning, entrepreneurial exploration, effective salary negotiation, continuous education, income diversification, networking efforts, and engagement in supplementary income activities, individuals can construct a resilient foundation for financial success.

Strategic Saving and Investment Approaches

Strategic approaches to saving and investing are fundamental to building wealth, demanding disciplined financial management and a forward-looking mindset to achieve enduring financial objectives.

1. Comprehensive Budgeting Practices

Implementing a thorough budget serves as the foundation for strategic financial planning. Categorizing income, allocating funds for essential expenses, and setting aside portions for savings and investments establish a clear financial roadmap.

Example: Utilize budgeting tools to monitor expenditures, create spending categories, and identify areas for potential savings.

2. Prioritizing the Emergency Fund

Giving priority to establishing an emergency fund is pivotal for financial resilience. This fund acts as a safety net, providing a financial buffer during unforeseen challenges and mitigating the necessity to tap into long-term investments or accrue high-interest debt.

Example: Strive to save an accessible emergency fund equivalent to three to six months' living expenses.

3. Diversifying Investment Portfolios

Constructing a diversified investment portfolio is essential for managing risk and optimizing returns. Allocating investments across various asset classes, such as stocks, bonds, and real estate, helps distribute risk and positions the portfolio for sustained growth.

Example: Seek advice from financial experts, explore investment options, and diversify holdings to create a well-balanced portfolio.

4. Consistent Contributions to Retirement Accounts

Making regular contributions to retirement accounts is a strategic move for long-term financial security. Employer-sponsored retirement plans and individual retirement accounts (IRAs) offer tax advantages and accumulate over time, significantly contributing to wealth accumulation.

Example: Maximize contributions to employer-sponsored 401(k) plans and consider additional contributions to individual IRAs.

5. Active Monitoring and Adjustments

Actively monitoring investment portfolios and financial goals is crucial, allowing for necessary adjustments as circumstances evolve. Regular reviews empower individuals to adapt to market changes, personal situations, and financial objectives.

Example: Periodically review investment performance, reassess financial goals, and make adjustments to contributions or portfolio allocations as needed.

6. Strategic Debt Management

Embracing strategic debt management practices is essential for financial well-being. Prioritizing high-interest debt repayment, avoiding unnecessary debt accumulation, and using debt strategically for investments with potential returns are key components.

Example: Formulate a debt repayment plan, prioritize debts with high interest rates, and consider consolidating debts for favourable terms.

7. Continuous Financial Education

Dedicating oneself to continuous financial education is vital for staying informed about investment strategies, economic trends, and financial planning. This ongoing learning ensures that individuals make informed decisions and adapt to the ever-evolving landscape of personal finance.

Example: Engage in financial literature, attend educational seminars, and enrol in online courses to enhance financial literacy and stay current with industry developments.

8. Automated Savings and Investments

Automating savings and investments streamlines the process, fostering consistency. Setting up automated transfers to savings accounts or investment portfolios eliminates the temptation to spend before saving, cultivating a disciplined savings habit.

Example: Schedule automatic transfers from a checking account to a savings or investment account on a regular basis.

9. Tax-Efficient Investment Strategies

Exploring tax-efficient investment strategies enhances returns and minimizes tax liabilities. Leveraging tax-advantaged accounts and optimizing investment structures based on tax implications contribute to overall financial efficiency.

Example: Consider tax-advantaged accounts like Roth IRAs, explore tax-loss harvesting strategies, and seek guidance from tax professionals for personalized advice.

In summary, adopting strategic saving and investment approaches involves meticulous budgeting, establishing emergency funds, diversifying portfolios, contributing to retirement accounts, active monitoring, debt management, continuous education, automated savings, and tax-efficient strategies. By incorporating these practices into a comprehensive financial plan, individuals can navigate the complexities of wealth accumulation with foresight and discipline.

Harnessing Growth Opportunities

Unlocking opportunities for growth is a dynamic endeavour that demands foresight, adaptability, and a proactive mindset. This section delves into key strategies for recognizing and capitalizing on opportunities that can propel financial success.

1. Spotting Investment Prospects

Proactively search for and identify investment prospects aligned with financial objectives. Whether in real estate, stocks, or business ventures, having a discerning eye for opportunities enables strategic capital deployment and the potential for substantial growth.

Example: Stay informed about market trends, conduct thorough due diligence, and seize opportunities demonstrating robust growth potential.

2. Cultivating Networks and Mentorship

Building a resilient professional network and pursuing mentorship opportunities are invaluable for uncovering new possibilities. Networking provides access to valuable connections, potential collaborations, and insights into lucrative opportunities. Mentorship offers guidance from experienced individuals who have successfully navigated the journey to wealth.

Example: Engage in industry events, become part of professional organizations, and actively seek mentorship from those with a proven track record in wealth creation.

3. Continuous Financial Learning

Commit to ongoing financial education to stay ahead of economic trends and investment strategies. Staying informed about emerging opportunities positions individuals to make informed decisions and adapt to evolving market conditions.

Example: Regularly consume financial publications, participate in seminars, and engage in webinars to stay updated on financial developments.

4. Strategic Debt Utilization

Embrace strategic debt utilization as a growth tool. While careful debt management is crucial, judiciously leveraging debt for investments like real estate or business expansion can expedite wealth-building. However, understanding and managing associated risks is essential.

Example: Evaluate potential return on investment when considering debt, and develop a repayment plan aligned with cash flow.

5. Fostering Innovation and Entrepreneurship

Explore innovation and entrepreneurship as avenues for growth. Identifying market gaps and developing innovative solutions can lead to successful ventures. Entrepreneurship provides opportunities to create value, generate additional income, and diversify revenue streams.

Example: Identify unmet needs in the market, brainstorm innovative solutions, and contemplate launching a business or product to address those needs.

6. Strategic Asset Diversification

Strategically diversify assets across various classes to optimize returns and manage risk effectively. A diversified portfolio in stocks, bonds, real estate, and other assets ensures balance and resilience in the face of market fluctuations.

Example: Consult financial advisors to determine the optimal asset diversification based on financial goals, risk tolerance, and market conditions.

7. Exploring Global Markets

Explore opportunities in global markets to diversify investments and tap into emerging trends. The interconnected nature of the global economy presents avenues for international investments that can yield substantial returns.

Example: Research and consider investing in international stocks, explore global real estate markets, and diversify exposure to different economies.

8. Adopting Technological Advancements

Stay abreast of technological advancements and integrate innovative tools to enhance financial strategies. Technological solutions can streamline processes, offer data-driven insights, and present new avenues for investment or business growth.

Example: Explore financial technology (fintech) solutions, incorporate digital platforms for investment analysis, and leverage technology to enhance overall financial management.

In conclusion, harnessing growth opportunities involves a proactive stance in recognizing investment prospects, cultivating networks, continuous education, strategic debt utilization, entrepreneurship, asset diversification, global market exploration, and technological adoption. By implementing these strategies, individuals position themselves to capitalize on opportunities and foster sustained financial growth.

Chapter 4: Surpassing the $10 Million Milestone

Reaching the significant $10 million milestone requires strategic manoeuvres, calculated risks, and a refined approach to wealth management. This section delves into essential strategies for scaling up, underscoring the significance of diversifying investments for long-term success, exploring entrepreneurial ventures for wealth acceleration, and adeptly managing risks and challenges.

Broadening Investments for Long-Term Success

1. Strategic Allocation of Assets

Strategically distribute assets across diverse classes to maximize returns and minimize risks. A methodical approach to asset allocation ensures a balanced portfolio capable of weathering market fluctuations and capitalizing on various market conditions.

Example: Regularly reassess asset allocation, considering factors such as market trends, economic indicators, and risk tolerance to make informed adjustments.

2. Innovative Real Estate Investment Strategies

Explore advanced real estate investment strategies for sustained growth. Beyond conventional property ownership, delve into options such as real estate investment trusts (REITs), real estate crowdfunding, and commercial properties to expand exposure and fortify the overall stability of your portfolio.

Example: Investigate emerging real estate markets, diversify property types, and consider innovative platforms for real estate investment.

3. Engagement with Private Equity

Consider engaging with private equity investments for opportunities not readily available in public markets. Participation in private companies or funds can provide access to high-growth potential ventures, albeit with increased risk. Rigorous due diligence and professional guidance are vital in navigating this terrain.

Example: Collaborate with private equity firms, conduct thorough due diligence on potential investments, and consider a diversified approach to mitigate risks.

4. Global Market Exploration

Expand investment horizons by exploring opportunities in global markets. International investments offer diversification benefits and exposure to industries and trends not prevalent in domestic markets.

Example: Investigate promising sectors in international markets, consider investing in global funds, and stay informed about geopolitical and economic factors influencing international investments.

5. Integration of Alternative Investments

Diversify further by incorporating alternative investments such as cryptocurrencies, precious metals, and hedge funds. While these carry their own set of risks, a well-balanced allocation to alternative investments can enhance portfolio resilience and capture uncorrelated returns.

Example: Allocate a modest portion of the portfolio to alternative investments, stay informed about market trends, and continually assess the risk-reward profile.

Entrepreneurial Ventures and Accelerated Wealth

1. Identification of Lucrative Business Avenues

Identify and capitalize on lucrative business opportunities to accelerate wealth accumulation. This could involve launching new ventures, acquiring established businesses, or investing in startups with substantial growth potential.

Example: Conduct thorough market research, assess industry trends, and identify niches where there is a demand for innovative solutions.

2. Strategic Partnerships and Collaborations

Explore strategic partnerships and collaborations to amplify entrepreneurial efforts. Collaborating with like-minded individuals or established businesses can provide access to resources, expertise, and market reach that accelerate the growth trajectory.

Example: Seek partnerships with complementary businesses, leverage shared resources, and negotiate mutually beneficial terms for collaborations.

3. Emphasis on Scalability and Innovation

Focus on scalability and innovation in entrepreneurial endeavours. Building a business with scalable models and a commitment to continuous innovation ensures sustained growth and opens avenues for attracting investors or going public.

Example: Regularly evaluate business processes for scalability, invest in research and development, and foster a culture of innovation within the organization.

4. Diversification of Business Holdings

Diversify entrepreneurial ventures by exploring different industries or sectors. Spreading business interests across diverse sectors mitigates risks associated with industry-specific downturns and broadens the potential for high returns.

Example: Consider expanding into industries with growth potential while maintaining a core focus on the primary business.

5. Implementation of Exit Strategies and Wealth Extraction Plans

Develop sound exit strategies to optimize wealth extraction from entrepreneurial ventures. Whether through selling the business, strategic mergers, or going public, having a well-thought-out exit plan ensures the realization of accumulated value.

Example: Collaborate with financial advisors to devise exit strategies aligned with business goals and market conditions.

Effectively Managing Risks and Challenges

1. Thorough Risk Assessment

Conduct a comprehensive risk assessment to identify potential challenges and mitigate their impact. Regularly reassess risks associated with investments, market fluctuations, and entrepreneurial ventures to proactively address emerging threats.

Example: Utilize risk management tools, conduct scenario analysis, and seek expert consultations to evaluate potential risks and formulate mitigation strategies.

2. Implementation of Wealth Protection Strategies

Implement effective wealth protection strategies to safeguard accumulated assets. This involves asset protection through legal structures, insurance coverage, and estate planning to ensure the seamless transfer of wealth to future generations.

Example: Engage legal professionals to establish trusts, regularly review insurance coverage, and update estate plans to reflect current circumstances.

3. Adoption of Adaptive Financial Planning

Embrace adaptive financial planning to navigate changing economic landscapes. A dynamic financial plan that adjusts to evolving market conditions and personal circumstances ensures resilience in the face of uncertainties.

Example: Regularly review financial plans, consider adjustments based on economic indicators, and remain agile in responding to changing financial goals.

4. Continuous Learning and Networking Initiatives

Stay informed through continuous learning and networking to anticipate challenges and opportunities. Networking with industry peers, staying abreast of market trends, and participating in professional development activities contribute to a proactive and informed approach to risk management.

Example: Attend industry conferences, engage in professional networks, and enrol in courses that enhance risk management skills.

5. Contingency Planning for Business Ventures

Develop comprehensive contingency plans for entrepreneurial ventures. Anticipating potential challenges, such as market disruptions or changes in consumer behaviour, and having predefined strategies for adaptation ensures business resilience.

Example: Formulate contingency plans that address various scenarios, including economic downturns, supply chain disruptions, or shifts in market demand.

In conclusion, surpassing the $10 million milestone requires a multifaceted approach, encompassing diversified investments, entrepreneurial ventures, and adept risk management. By strategically allocating assets, exploring entrepreneurial opportunities, and proactively managing risks, individuals can propel themselves toward sustained financial success and navigate the complexities of wealth at a higher level.

Chapter 5: Breaking Through the Nine-Figure Barrier

Achieving the coveted nine-figure net worth requires a blend of innovation, strategic networking, and overcoming mental hurdles. This section explores key strategies for breaking through the nine-figure barrier, emphasizing the significance of innovating in business and investments, creating and nurturing high-value networks, and conquering mental blocks to reach unparalleled financial heights.

Innovating in Business and Investments
1. Integration of Disruptive Technologies

Embrace the transformative potential of disruptive technologies by actively incorporating them into your business strategies. Technologies like artificial intelligence, blockchain, and the Internet of Things can revolutionize processes, boost efficiency, and open up new avenues for revenue.

Example: Implement machine learning algorithms to optimize business operations, explore blockchain applications for secure and transparent transactions, and leverage IoT devices for data-driven insights.

2. Agility in Business Models

Adopt agile business models that enable swift adaptation to changing market conditions. Flexibility and responsiveness are essential for navigating the dynamic business landscape, allowing your enterprise to quickly seize emerging opportunities.

Example: Implement agile project management methodologies, foster a culture of continuous improvement, and remain receptive to pivoting business models based on market feedback.

3. Commitment to Eco-Friendly Practices

Incorporate eco-friendly and sustainable practices into your business operations. Beyond meeting societal expectations for environmental responsibility, this approach can attract environmentally conscious consumers and investors, creating a positive impact on both your business and the planet.

<u>Example:</u> Implement energy-efficient technologies, adopt sustainable supply chain practices, and actively communicate your commitment to environmental responsibility to stakeholders.

4. Embracing Open Innovation Frameworks

Promote open innovation by collaborating with external partners, startups, and research institutions. Open innovation frameworks can lead to breakthrough ideas, fresh perspectives, and the identification of untapped market opportunities.

Example: Establish partnerships with startups for collaborative projects, sponsor innovation challenges to attract external talent, and actively participate in industry-wide collaborations.

5. Customer-Centric Product Development

Place a strong emphasis on customer-centric product development by actively seeking and incorporating customer feedback. Understanding customer needs and preferences ensures that your products and services stay relevant and meet the evolving demands of the market.

Example: Conduct regular surveys, solicit customer feedback through various channels, and use data analytics to gain insights into customer behaviour for informed decision-making.

6. Strategic Diversification

Explore diversification strategies to expand your business portfolio. Diversifying into new markets, industries, or product lines can mitigate risks, create additional revenue streams, and position your business for sustained growth.

Example: Conduct market research to identify growth opportunities, assess the feasibility of diversification initiatives, and develop a strategic plan for entering new markets.

7. Harnessing Data Analytics Effectively

Leverage the power of data analytics to make informed business decisions. Utilizing big data and analytics tools enables you to derive actionable insights, optimize processes, and identify trends that can inform strategic moves.

Example: Implement data analytics tools to analyse customer behaviour, forecast market trends, and enhance operational efficiency based on data-driven insights.

8. Revolutionizing Marketing Strategies

Revamp traditional marketing strategies with innovative approaches to capture audience attention. Leveraging social media, influencer marketing, and interactive content can create a strong brand presence and drive customer engagement.

Example: Utilize social media platforms for targeted advertising, collaborate with influencers to reach specific demographics, and experiment with interactive content like augmented reality experiences.

9. Prioritizing Continuous Employee Development

Invest in ongoing training and development programs for employees. Ensuring that your workforce is equipped with the latest skills and knowledge fosters a culture of innovation within the organization.

Example: Provide regular training sessions on emerging technologies, encourage employees to pursue professional development courses, and create a culture that values learning and experimentation.

In summary, fostering innovation in business and investments entails embracing disruptive technologies, cultivating agile business models, committing to eco-friendly practices, promoting open innovation, prioritizing customer-centric product development, strategically diversifying, harnessing data analytics, revolutionizing marketing, and investing in continuous employee development. Through these approaches, businesses can position themselves as leaders, stay adaptable in a rapidly evolving landscape, and drive sustainable growth.

Building and Sustaining Valuable Networks

1. Methodical Relationship Cultivation

Foster high-value networks through systematic relationship cultivation. Develop meaningful connections with influential figures, industry leaders, and decision-makers by actively participating in industry events, engaging in targeted networking, and understanding the goals and aspirations of potential key contacts.

Example: Attend exclusive industry conferences, take part in leadership forums, and establish individual connections with key stakeholders in your field.

2. Initiating Collaborative Endeavours

Initiate and foster collaborations proactively. High-value networks thrive on collaboration, be it through joint ventures, shared projects, or mutual support. Identifying opportunities for collaboration and demonstrating a commitment to collective success can significantly enhance the value of your network.

Example: Propose collaborative projects with industry peers, share resources, and actively seek chances to support and uplift fellow professionals.

3. Creation of Advisory Boards

Consider forming advisory boards with seasoned professionals. Advisory boards offer diverse expertise and insights, providing valuable guidance for crucial decisions. The relationships established within these boards contribute to a robust high-value network.

Example: Assemble an advisory board with members possessing expertise in various aspects of your industry, convene regular meetings for strategic discussions, and leverage the collective wisdom of the board.

4. Investment in Personal Reputation

Invest in personal branding to augment your influence within high-value networks. Cultivating a strong personal brand not only attracts attention but also builds credibility and trust. Actively curate your online presence, share thought leadership content, and consistently communicate your professional values.

Example: Develop a personal brand strategy, contribute insightful content through blogs or social media, and actively engage with your audience to build a positive online reputation.

5. Participation in Exclusive Forums

Engage in exclusive industry forums and memberships. Joining elite groups provides access to decision-makers and influencers. These forums often facilitate intimate discussions, allowing you to share your expertise and gain insights from other accomplished professionals.

Example: Apply for memberships in industry-specific associations, participate in closed-door forums, and contribute meaningfully to discussions within these exclusive circles.

6. Strategic Mentorship Connections

Forge strategic mentorship relationships with accomplished individuals. Mentorship not only provides valuable guidance but also connects you with an influential network through your mentor's own connections. Seek mentors whose experiences align with your goals and aspirations.

Example: Identify potential mentors within your industry, approach them with a clear mentorship proposal, and actively seek their advice and insights.

7. Active Engagement in Philanthropy

Participate actively in philanthropy and community initiatives. Active involvement in philanthropy not only contributes to societal well-being but also connects you with like-minded individuals who share a passion for making a positive impact.

Example: Establish or contribute to charitable foundations, engage in community service projects, and attend philanthropic events to connect with socially conscious professionals.

8. Reciprocal Value Generation

Prioritize reciprocal value creation within your network. Actively look for opportunities to provide value to your connections, whether through introductions, sharing insights, or offering support. A network built on reciprocal value creation strengthens over time.

Example: Actively seek ways to assist your connections, make strategic introductions, and share valuable resources that align with the needs of individuals within your network.

9. Cross-Industry Networking

Extend your networking efforts beyond your immediate industry. Diversifying your connections across various sectors broadens your perspective, introduces you to fresh ideas, and opens doors to unexpected opportunities.

Example: Attend cross-industry events, explore collaborations with professionals from different sectors, and actively seek networking opportunities beyond your industry boundaries.

In summary, building and sustaining valuable networks involve systematic relationship cultivation, proactive collaboration initiatives, the establishment of advisory boards, investment in personal branding, participation in industry forums, strategic mentorship relationships, active engagement in philanthropy, prioritizing reciprocal value creation, and cross-industry networking. Adopting these practices enables individuals to cultivate robust networks that significantly contribute to personal and professional growth.

Conquering Mental Hurdles on the Path to Financial Success

1. Fostering Resilience Amidst Challenges

Cultivate resilience as a foundational quality for surmounting mental obstacles. Financial journeys often present challenges, and developing resilience enables individuals to bounce back from setbacks, extract lessons from failures, and persistently move forward toward their financial objectives.

Example: Embrace challenges as opportunities for growth, reflect on past setbacks to extract valuable insights, and approach obstacles with a mindset geared towards resilience.

2. Nurturing Emotional Intelligence

Invest in nurturing emotional intelligence to effectively navigate financial complexities. Understanding and managing personal and financial emotions enhances the ability to make rational choices, withstand market fluctuations, and maintain a clear focus on long-term financial goals.

Example: Practice self-awareness to recognize emotional triggers, employ effective stress management techniques, and seek feedback from trusted mentors to enhance emotional intelligence.

3. Positive Visualization and Confirmations

Integrate positive visualization and confirmations into daily practices. Visualizing financial success and consistently affirming positive beliefs can rewire the mind, fostering a constructive outlook and reinforcing the belief in reaching financial heights.

Example: Create a visual representation of financial goals, engage in daily visualization exercises, and develop personalized affirmations that align with your aspirations.

4. Setting Realistic Goals Strategically

Establish strategic and attainable financial goals. Breaking down long-term objectives into manageable milestones aids in maintaining focus and alleviates the pressure associated with aiming for monumental success. Celebrate smaller victories along the journey.

Example: Set clear and measurable financial goals, create a step-by-step action plan to achieve them, and regularly assess progress to stay motivated.

5. Embracing Continuous Learning and Adaptation

Adopt a mindset of continuous learning and adaptation. Financial landscapes evolve, and being open to acquiring new knowledge, staying updated on market trends, and adjusting strategies positions individuals to navigate uncertainties confidently.

Example: Enrol in financial literacy courses, read industry publications, and actively seek mentorship to stay informed and adaptable in the ever-changing financial environment.

6. Incorporating Mindfulness Practices

Incorporate mindfulness practices to manage stress and enhance focus. Techniques like meditation and mindful breathing contribute to mental clarity, reducing anxiety associated with financial decisions and fostering a calm and collected approach.

Example: Integrate brief mindfulness sessions into daily routines, practice mindful breathing during stressful financial situations, and prioritize moments of quiet reflection.

7. Prioritizing Financial Planning and Education

Allocate time to comprehensive financial planning and education. Understanding financial principles, budgeting, and investment strategies empowers individuals to make informed decisions, mitigating anxiety related to financial uncertainty.

Example: Attend financial planning workshops, consult with financial advisors for personalized guidance, and stay informed about various investment options.

8. Building Support Systems and Seeking Professional Guidance

Cultivate strong support systems and seek professional guidance. Surrounding oneself with a supportive network, including mentors, friends, and family, provides emotional reinforcement. Additionally, consulting financial professionals contributes to informed decision-making.

Example: Foster relationships with like-minded individuals who share financial goals, seek advice from financial advisors, and actively engage in discussions with trusted mentors.

9. Incorporating Gratitude Practices

Integrate gratitude practices to maintain a positive perspective. Reflecting on achievements, expressing gratitude for financial progress, and acknowledging abundance in one's life contribute to a positive mindset, counteracting feelings of scarcity or inadequacy.

Example: Maintain a gratitude journal, regularly acknowledge financial achievements, and express gratitude for opportunities and resources available.

In summary, conquering mental hurdles on the path to financial success involves cultivating resilience, nurturing emotional intelligence, practicing positive visualization, setting realistic goals strategically, embracing continuous learning, incorporating mindfulness, prioritizing financial planning and education, building support systems, and integrating gratitude practices. By adopting these strategies, individuals can develop a resilient mindset that propels them toward financial heights with confidence and a positive outlook.

Chapter 6 Sustaining and Growing Wealth

Legacy Planning and Safeguarding Family Wealth

1. Strategic Estate Planning

In the pursuit of sustaining and growing wealth, strategic estate planning takes centre stage. Develop a comprehensive plan that addresses inheritance, tax implications, and the seamless transition of assets to the next generation. This not only preserves wealth but also ensures a lasting legacy.

Example: Engage with legal and financial professionals to create a robust estate plan that includes wills, trusts, and other instruments to safeguard assets and minimize tax liabilities for future generations.

2. Family Governance Structures

Establishing family governance structures is pivotal for sustaining wealth across generations. Create family constitutions and structures that outline shared values, responsibilities, and decision-making processes. This fosters unity and collaboration, safeguarding the family's financial legacy.

Example: Develop a family constitution that articulates financial principles, appoint family councils for decision-making, and conduct regular family meetings to reinforce a sense of shared responsibility.

3. Philanthropic Initiatives

Incorporating philanthropic initiatives into legacy planning adds a meaningful dimension. Create foundations, trusts, or charitable organizations that align with family values. Giving back not only contributes to societal well-being but also reinforces a positive family legacy.

Example: Establish a family foundation supporting causes aligned with shared values, actively involve family members in philanthropic efforts, and explore innovative ways to contribute to social impact.

4. Asset Protection Strategies

Implementing asset protection strategies is crucial for wealth preservation. Shield assets from potential risks through legal structures and insurance. This proactive approach safeguards the family's financial foundation and ensures the continuity of generational wealth.

Example: Utilize trusts, limited liability entities, and insurance products to protect assets from litigation, creditors, and unforeseen financial challenges.

5. Diversification and Risk Management

Diversifying investments and implementing effective risk management strategies are key elements in wealth preservation. Balancing a portfolio across different asset classes mitigates risks and ensures resilience in varying economic conditions, contributing to sustained growth.

Example: Regularly review and rebalance investment portfolios, consider alternative investments for diversification, and employ risk management strategies to protect against market fluctuations.

6.   Effective   Communication   Across Generations

Establishing transparent communication strategies across generations is pivotal for comprehensive legacy planning. Encourage open discussions about wealth, values, and expectations, fostering a shared understanding that aligns the family's legacy with collective aspirations.

Example: Facilitate regular family meetings for financial discussions, provide financial education to younger family members, and create a platform for inter-generational dialogue on preserving family wealth.

7. Documentation of Family Narratives and Values

Preserving wealth extends beyond financial assets to encompass family narratives and values. Documenting the family's history, values, and significant milestones contributes to a rich legacy. This archival approach provides a narrative that enhances the emotional connection to wealth and reinforces family identity.

Example: Compile a family archive with written and oral histories, construct a family tree, and encourage storytelling sessions to pass down collective wisdom and values to future generations.

8. Strategic Succession Planning for Business Enterprises

For families with businesses, meticulous succession planning is imperative. Develop a comprehensive plan for the transfer of leadership roles and ownership. This ensures a seamless transition, minimizes disruptions, and upholds the integrity of the family business as a cornerstone of the family's legacy.

Example: Engage with succession planning experts, clearly define roles and responsibilities for family members, and establish a gradual transition plan that allows successors to gain experience and expertise.

9. Integration of Philanthropy into the Family Legacy

Infusing philanthropy into legacy planning introduces a philanthropic dimension. Establishing a family foundation, creating charitable trusts, or contributing to impactful causes becomes a lasting legacy that extends beyond financial wealth. This approach aligns the family's legacy with positive societal contributions.

Example: Engage family members in discussions about philanthropy, jointly decide on charitable causes, and integrate philanthropic initiatives into the family's long-term legacy plan.

10. Utilization of Legal Frameworks for Wealth Transfer

Implementing robust legal structures is fundamental to wealth preservation. Employ tools like trusts, family limited partnerships, and foundations to facilitate a smooth transfer of assets while minimizing tax implications. These legal frameworks provide a solid foundation for preserving family wealth across generations.

Example: Collaborate with legal professionals to establish trusts aligned with family goals, explore family limited partnerships for efficient asset transfer, and consider the creation of a family foundation for philanthropic endeavours.

11. Promotion of Financial Stewardship Education

Instilling a sense of responsibility and financial literacy in family members is integral to wealth preservation. Conduct financial education workshops, encourage the pursuit of relevant qualifications in finance, and mentor younger family members to ensure future generations are equipped to manage and grow family wealth responsibly.

Example: Facilitate financial education workshops for family members, encourage the pursuit of relevant qualifications in finance, and mentor younger family members on effective financial stewardship.

12. Regular Evaluation and Adjustment of Legacy Plans

Legacy plans are dynamic and should undergo regular evaluation and adjustment. Economic conditions, family dynamics, and societal changes can impact the effectiveness of legacy planning. Regular reviews ensure that the plan remains relevant and aligned with evolving circumstances.

Example: Conduct periodic reviews of legacy plans, involve family members in the review process, and make adjustments based on changing circumstances or emerging family goals.

In summary, comprehensive legacy planning involves transparent communication, documentation of family narratives, strategic succession planning for businesses, integration of philanthropy, utilization of legal frameworks, financial stewardship education, and regular evaluations of legacy plans. This holistic approach ensures that the family's wealth endures not only in financial terms but also in the values, narratives, and positive impact passed down through generations.

Continuous Learning and Adaptation
1. Staying Informed in a Dynamic Landscape

Wealth sustenance requires an unwavering commitment to continuous learning. Stay informed about economic trends, market dynamics, and emerging opportunities. Adapting to the ever-evolving financial landscape positions individuals and families for sustained success.

Example: Engage in ongoing education through financial seminars, subscribe to reputable financial publications, and leverage digital platforms for real-time updates on market trends.

2. Embracing Technological Advancements

Embrace technological advancements to enhance financial acumen. Leverage fintech solutions, digital platforms, and artificial intelligence tools for efficient wealth management. Integrating technology not only streamlines processes but also opens avenues for innovative investment strategies.

Example: Utilize robo-advisors for automated investment management, explore blockchain-based investment platforms, and stay abreast of technological trends shaping the financial industry.

3. Networking and Collaboration

Actively engage in networking and collaborative initiatives to stay ahead in the financial landscape. Connect with industry experts, fellow investors, and thought leaders to exchange insights and explore collaborative ventures. Networking provides access to diverse perspectives and potential opportunities.

Example: Attend industry conferences, join professional associations, and participate in collaborative projects that involve knowledge sharing and networking within the financial community.

4. Adapting Investment Strategies

Adapting investment strategies in response to market shifts is fundamental for sustained growth. Regularly reassess investment goals, risk tolerance, and financial objectives. Flexibility in adjusting strategies based on changing circumstances ensures relevance and effectiveness.

Example: Shift allocations based on changing market conditions, consider emerging sectors for investment, and be agile in adjusting the investment portfolio to align with evolving financial goals.

5. Educational Initiatives for Future Generations

Extend the commitment to continuous learning to future generations. Implement educational initiatives within the family to equip heirs with financial literacy. This empowers the next generation to actively participate in wealth management and ensures a seamless transition of financial knowledge.

Example: Establish financial literacy programs for family members, provide mentorship opportunities, and encourage the pursuit of relevant educational qualifications in finance and economics.

6. Leveraging Technological Advancements

Remaining open to continuous learning involves leveraging technological advancements to stay current with industry progress. Engage in online courses, webinars, and educational platforms to gain up-to-date knowledge. Embracing emerging technologies not only enhances financial expertise but also positions individuals to utilize innovative solutions in managing wealth.

Example: Enrol in online courses covering fintech, participate in webinars discussing blockchain and artificial intelligence, and explore digital platforms providing real-time insights into market trends.

7. Exploring New Investment Avenues

Continuous learning extends to exploring fresh investment opportunities. Stay informed about emerging markets, industries, and investment prospects. Adjusting investment strategies to incorporate these new opportunities ensures a diversified portfolio and the potential for significant returns.

Example: Investigate and consider investments in emerging sectors, stay informed about global economic trends, and think about diversifying your investment portfolio to include promising opportunities.

8. Networking for Insights and Collaborations

Actively participate in networking for valuable insights and collaborative ventures. Connect with industry experts, fellow investors, and professionals to share ideas and explore potential collaborations. Networking not only broadens perspectives but also opens doors to strategic partnerships and innovative projects.

Example: Attend industry conferences, join investment forums, and engage in collaborative initiatives that facilitate knowledge exchange and networking within the financial community.

9. Adapting to Regulatory Changes

In the ever-evolving financial landscape, staying abreast of regulatory changes is essential. Continuous learning involves understanding shifts in financial regulations and adjusting strategies to comply with new standards. Proactively adapting to regulatory changes mitigates risks and ensures financial practices remain in line with evolving regulatory landscapes.

Example: Keep track of financial regulations through regular monitoring of updates, seek legal advice to interpret changes, and modify financial strategies to align with evolving regulatory environments.

10. Investing in Skill Enhancement

Investing in skill enhancement is a fundamental aspect of continuous learning. Acquire and refine skills relevant to financial management, data analysis, and decision-making. Continuous improvement ensures individuals remain competitive and capable of navigating complex financial scenarios.

Example: Obtain certifications in financial analysis, data science, or risk management, attend skill-building workshops, and actively pursue opportunities to enhance analytical and decision-making skills.

11. Cultivating a Growth Mindset

Fostering a growth mindset is crucial for continuous learning. Embrace challenges as learning opportunities, persist in the face of setbacks, and view failures as stepping stones toward improvement. A growth mindset promotes resilience, adaptability, and a proactive approach to continuous self-improvement.

Example: Approach challenges with a positive mindset, seek feedback for personal growth, and perceive setbacks as valuable learning experiences contributing to professional and personal development.

12. Maintaining Awareness of Global Economics

Continuous learning involves staying informed about global economic trends. Keep abreast of geopolitical events, economic indicators, and international market dynamics. Understanding the interconnectedness of global economies enhances the ability to make informed financial decisions in a rapidly changing world.

Example: Regularly read international financial publications, monitor global economic indicators, and participate in forums or webinars offering insights into the global economic landscape.

In summary, continuous learning and adaptation include leveraging technological advancements, exploring new investment opportunities, networking for insights, adapting to regulatory changes, investing in skill enhancement, cultivating a growth mindset, and staying aware of global economic trends. This proactive approach ensures individuals remain flexible, well-informed, and adept at navigating the dynamic terrain of financial management.

Giving Back and Contributing to Society
1. Strategic Philanthropy for Impact

Integrating philanthropy into wealth management involves strategic planning for impactful giving. Identify causes that resonate with family values and allocate resources in a way that maximizes positive social impact. Strategic philanthropy not only contributes to society but also shapes the family's legacy positively.

Example: Collaborate with philanthropic advisors, conduct thorough research on potential beneficiaries, and allocate funds strategically to initiatives aligned with the family's values and goals.

2. Creating Sustainable Social Programs

Contributing to society involves creating sustainable social programs. Establish initiatives that address systemic issues and contribute to long-term positive change. This approach aligns philanthropy with the family's commitment to making a lasting impact on societal challenges.

Example: Develop social programs that focus on education, healthcare, or environmental sustainability, ensuring that initiatives have a lasting impact and contribute to positive social change.

3. Encouraging Social Responsibility Across Generations

Instilling a sense of social responsibility across generations is integral. Engage family members in philanthropic decision-making, encouraging them to actively participate in identifying and supporting social causes. This cultivates a culture of giving back within the family.

Example: Hold family meetings to discuss philanthropic initiatives, involve younger family members in decision-making processes, and celebrate collective contributions to societal well-being.

4. Measuring and Evaluating Impact

A commitment to contributing to society involves measuring and evaluating the impact of philanthropic efforts. Implement metrics and assessment tools to gauge the effectiveness of social initiatives. This data-driven approach ensures that resources are directed where they can create the most positive change.

Example: Collaborate with impact assessment experts, establish key performance indicators for philanthropic programs, and regularly evaluate the outcomes and effectiveness of social initiatives.

5. Collaboration with Non-profit Organizations

Collaborating with reputable non-profit organizations enhances the effectiveness of philanthropic endeavours. Partnering with established entities ensures that resources are channelled efficiently, and initiatives are aligned with best practices in the non-profit sector.

Example: Identify and collaborate with well-established non-profit organizations, participate in joint initiatives, and leverage the expertise of non-profits to amplify the impact of philanthropic contributions.

6. Collaborative Partnerships with Non-profit Organizations

Engaging in collaborative partnerships with non-profits enhances the effectiveness of philanthropic endeavours. Identify reputable organizations aligned with family values and collaborate on initiatives addressing societal challenges. These alliances amplify the impact of contributions, directing resources where they can create the most meaningful change.

Example: Form alliances with established non-profits pursuing shared objectives, participate in joint initiatives, and leverage the expertise of non-profit organizations to maximize the effectiveness of philanthropic contributions.

7. Supporting Educational Initiatives for Empowerment

Contributing to society involves endorsing educational initiatives that empower individuals and communities. Invest in programs facilitating access to quality education, vocational training, and skill development. By enabling educational opportunities, philanthropy becomes a catalyst for sustained positive transformation.

Example: Sponsor scholarships, fund educational programs in underserved communities, and support initiatives promoting skill development, empowering individuals to build sustainable futures.

8. Projects for Environmental Sustainability

Incorporating environmental sustainability into philanthropy contributes to a healthier planet. Back initiatives focused on conservation, renewable energy, and sustainable practices. By championing environmental causes, philanthropy becomes a force for positive change that extends beyond immediate societal needs.

Example: Contribute to reforestation projects, finance research on sustainable energy solutions, and support organizations dedicated to promoting eco-friendly practices for a more sustainable future.

9. Community Development and Infrastructure Investments

Philanthropy can play a pivotal role in community development and infrastructure enhancement. Invest in projects improving the well-being of communities, such as constructing schools, healthcare facilities, or community centres. These contributions establish lasting structures benefiting society for generations.

Example: Fund construction projects for community infrastructure, collaborate with local authorities to enhance public amenities, and contribute to initiatives uplifting the overall well-being of communities.

10. Enhancing Healthcare Access and Supporting Medical Research

Supporting healthcare access and medical research addresses critical societal needs. Contribute to projects improving healthcare infrastructure, providing medical assistance to underserved populations, and funding research initiatives advancing medical knowledge. Such philanthropy directly contributes to the well-being of communities.

Example: Fund mobile healthcare clinics for underserved areas, support medical research institutions developing ground-breaking treatments, and collaborate with healthcare organizations to improve access to quality medical services.

11. Promoting Ventures in Social Entrepreneurship

Promoting ventures in social entrepreneurship aligns philanthropy with sustainable solutions.

Invest in initiatives addressing societal challenges through innovative business models. This approach provides financial support while fostering self-sufficiency and long-term positive impact.

Example: Support social enterprises blending profit with a social mission, invest in businesses tackling social issues, and mentor entrepreneurs dedicated to creating positive societal change through their ventures.

12. Measuring and Communicating Social Impact

A commitment to giving back involves measuring and communicating the social impact of philanthropic initiatives. Implement metrics and reporting mechanisms to assess the effectiveness of contributions. This data-driven approach ensures transparency, accountability, and the ability to refine strategies for maximum societal benefit.

Example: Collaborate with experts in impact assessment, establish key performance indicators for philanthropic programs, and regularly report on the outcomes and effectiveness of social initiatives.

In summary, engaging in philanthropy and contributing to society entails forming collaborative partnerships with nonprofits, endorsing educational initiatives, supporting environmental sustainability, investing in community development, enhancing healthcare access, promoting social entrepreneurship, and measuring the social impact of philanthropic efforts. This comprehensive approach ensures philanthropy becomes a catalyst for positive change, addressing diverse societal needs and leaving a lasting legacy of impact and compassion.

Chapter 7: Case Studies

Profiles of Individuals Who Achieved Nine-Figure Success

1. Warren Buffett: The Oracle of Omaha

Known for his disciplined investment approach, Warren Buffett's journey from a small investor to one of the globe's wealthiest individuals is a testament to long-term value investing. Analysing his strategies, including a focus on intrinsic value and a patient approach, provides invaluable insights for wealth accumulation.

Key Takeaways: Embrace long-term investment strategies, prioritize intrinsic value, and maintain patience in navigating market fluctuations.

2. Oprah Winfrey: Media Tycoon and Humanitarian

Oprah Winfrey's trajectory from a challenging upbringing to becoming a media icon showcases the power of resilience and authenticity. Examining her philanthropic endeavours emphasizes the importance of giving back and leveraging success for positive societal impact.

Key Takeaways: Cultivate resilience, authenticity, and actively contribute to societal well-being as part of success.

3. Elon Musk: Visionary Innovator and Entrepreneur

Elon Musk's ventures in technology, renewable energy, and space exploration highlight the impact of visionary thinking. His risk-taking approach and commitment to transformative projects illustrate the role of innovation in achieving substantial financial success.

Key Takeaways: Embrace visionary thinking, be willing to take calculated risks, and invest in ground-breaking innovations.

4. Sara Blakely: Disrupting Fashion with Spanx

As the founder of Spanx, Sara Blakely disrupted the fashion industry and built a billion-dollar empire. Her entrepreneurial journey underscores the importance of identifying market gaps, pursuing unique solutions, and persisting through challenges.

Key Takeaways: Identify market opportunities, innovate in product development, and persevere through entrepreneurial challenges.

5. Bill Gates: Tech Pioneer Turned Philanthropist

Bill Gates' transition from a tech pioneer at Microsoft to a leading philanthropist at the Bill & Melinda Gates Foundation showcases the impact of leveraging wealth for social good. His commitment to addressing global issues highlights the potential for using financial success to make a lasting positive impact.

Key Takeaways: Strategically leverage wealth for philanthropy, address global challenges, and contribute to societal betterment.

Lessons Drawn from Real-Life Success Narratives

1. Adaptability in Evolving Markets

Examining various success stories underscores the importance of adaptability in changing markets. Individuals who achieved nine-figure success often demonstrated the ability to pivot, adjust strategies, and identify new opportunities in response to evolving economic landscapes.

Key Insights: Foster adaptability, regularly reassess strategies, and be open to innovation in response to changing market dynamics.

2. Strategic Networking and Collaborations

Successful individuals consistently emphasize the significance of strategic networking and collaborations. Building strong professional relationships, seeking mentorship, and engaging in collaborative ventures contribute significantly to long-term success.

Key Insights: Prioritize networking, seek mentorship opportunities, and explore collaborations to enhance professional growth.

3. Continuous Learning and Skill Enhancement

The theme of continuous learning is a common thread in the success stories analysed. Individuals who reached nine-figure success demonstrated a commitment to ongoing education, skill development, and staying informed about industry trends.

Key Insights: Embrace a commitment to continuous learning, invest in skill development, and stay informed about industry advancements.

4. Risk Management and Resilience

The case studies underscore the importance of effective risk management and resilience. Successful individuals navigated challenges with a resilient mindset, effectively mitigated risks, and viewed setbacks as opportunities for growth.

Key Insights: Develop robust risk management strategies, cultivate resilience in the face of challenges, and view setbacks as learning opportunities.

5. Philanthropy as a Core Value

Philanthropy emerges as a recurring theme among those who achieved significant success. Integrating philanthropy as a core value not only contributes to societal well-being but also adds depth and purpose to financial success.

Key Insights: Embed philanthropy as a core value, actively contribute to societal betterment, and use wealth to create positive social impact.

6. Innovation and Visionary Thinking

Innovation and visionary thinking are pivotal elements in the success stories studied.

Individuals who achieved nine-figure success often demonstrated the ability to think beyond conventional boundaries, innovate in their fields, and pursue transformative ideas.

Key Insights: Foster innovation, embrace visionary thinking, and pursue transformative ideas to stand out in competitive landscapes.

7. Balancing Ambition with Ethical Business Practices

The case studies highlight the importance of balancing ambition with ethical business practices. Achieving nine-figure success is not solely about financial gains but also about maintaining ethical standards, integrity, and a commitment to positive business conduct.

Key Insights: Prioritize ethical business practices, maintain integrity, and balance ambition with responsible corporate behaviour.

This exploration of case studies provides a nuanced understanding of individuals who achieved nine-figure success and distils key lessons learned from their real-life success stories. From the disciplined investing approach of Warren Buffett to the disruptive entrepreneurship of Sara Blakely, each case

study offers unique insights that can inform and
inspire those on the path to financial success.

Chapter 8: Actionable Strategies

Step-by-Step Exercises and Action Plans

1. Strategic Financial Goal Setting

Exercise:

Commence by envisioning your long-term financial objectives, breaking them down into smaller, achievable milestones such as homeownership, education funding, or retirement planning.

Action Plan:

Construct a detailed timeline for each milestone, outlining specific steps and tasks required for attainment. Regularly review and adjust your plan to adapt to evolving circumstances and priorities.

2. Precision in Budgeting

Exercise:

Scrutinize your monthly expenses for at least one month, categorizing each expenditure. Identify spending patterns and pinpoint areas where adjustments are possible.

Action Plan:

Develop a realistic budget, allocating funds to various categories, including savings and investments. Consistently review and refine your budget, utilizing tools or apps for efficiency.

3. Strategies for Effective Debt Management

Exercise:

Catalog all outstanding debts, categorizing them by interest rates and terms. Gain a comprehensive understanding of total indebtedness and monthly payment commitments.

Action Plan:

Prioritize debt repayment, starting with high-interest debts. Explore consolidation options and negotiate with creditors for improved terms. Construct a repayment plan synchronized with your budget.

4. Evaluation of Investment Readiness

Exercise:

Assess your risk tolerance, considering your comfort level with market fluctuations. Define financial goals and gauge your investment knowledge and experience.

Action Plan:

Diversify your investment portfolio based on the assessment. Research various investment avenues and seek guidance from financial professionals for a comprehensive and risk-aligned strategy.

5. Exploration of Income Enhancement

Exercise:

Identify skills or talents with monetization potential. Explore additional income streams, such as freelance work or side businesses.

Action Plan:

Invest time in developing marketable skills and explore opportunities for freelance work or side businesses. Formulate a gradual plan to increase income streams, contributing to overall financial growth.

These systematic exercises and corresponding action plans offer a robust framework for readers to actively manage their financial affairs. By setting precise goals, practicing effective budgeting, strategically managing debts, making informed investment choices, and exploring avenues for income enhancement, individuals can navigate their financial journey with confidence and purpose.

Empowering Tools and Resources for Financial Advancement

Enhanced Financial Tracking Applications

Tools:

Utilize sophisticated financial tracking applications like **Mint or YNAB** for real-time insights into spending habits, effective budgeting, and tracking progress towards financial objectives.

Resources:

Explore comprehensive tutorials and user guides provided by these applications to unlock their full potential. Engage in forums or communities associated with these tools for additional tips and insights.

Strategic Investment Platforms and Automated Advisors

Tools:

Engage with user-friendly investment platforms such as **Robinhood or Vanguard.** Consider the convenience of robo-advisors like Wealth front or Betterment for automated and diversified investment strategies.

Resources:

Immerse yourself in educational materials offered by these platforms. Develop a solid understanding of investment principles, portfolio management, and risk assessment for making well-informed financial decisions.

Online Learning Platforms for Skill Enhancement

Tools:

Explore the vast selection of online learning platforms, such as **Coursera or LinkedIn**

Learning, to acquire new skills essential for professional and financial growth.

Resources:

Delve into courses related to finance, entrepreneurship, and personal development. Leverage supplementary resources like forums and community discussions for practical insights and networking opportunities.

Financial Calculators and Planning Tools

Tools:

Access financial calculators designed for retirement planning, loan repayments, and investment projections to guide strategic financial decision-making.

Resources:

Discover websites offering comprehensive financial planning tools. Familiarize yourself with effective usage through user guides and educational content provided by the respective platforms.

Stay Informed with Economic News Outlets

Tools:

Subscribe to reputable financial news outlets and analysis platforms for staying abreast of market trends, economic indicators, and global financial developments.

Resources:

Delve into detailed analyses and reports provided by these platforms. Participate in webinars or virtual events organized by these outlets to gain insights from financial experts.

These cutting-edge tools and resources serve as a dynamic toolkit for individuals seeking financial growth. By embracing advanced tracking apps, strategic investment platforms, continuous skill development, financial calculators, and staying informed through reputable news outlets, readers can actively steer their financial journey towards sustained advancement.

Nurturing a Supportive Network for Achievement

1. Engaging in Mentorship and Networking Circles

Action Steps:

Initiate connections with seasoned individuals in your field for mentorship. Actively participate in professional networking groups to broaden your sphere of influence.

Plan:

Attend industry events, virtual meetups, and conferences to establish meaningful relationships. Seek guidance from mentors to navigate challenges and capitalize on growth opportunities.

2. Exploring Financial Advisory Services

Action Steps:

Consider engaging a financial advisor for personalized guidance aligned with your distinct financial goals and circumstances.

Plan:

Conduct thorough research to identify a financial advisor matching your aspirations. Arrange consultations to discuss your financial plan, investment strategies, and long-term objectives.

3. Forming Peer Accountability Alliances

Action Steps:

Establish partnerships with peers who share similar financial aspirations. Regularly check in, exchange goals, and offer mutual support.

Plan:

Organize structured meetings to review progress, address challenges, and set goals. Utilize each other's strengths to enhance accountability and celebrate collective successes.

4. Active Participation in Online Communities and Forums

Action Steps:

Engage proactively in online communities and forums related to finance and entrepreneurship. Share experiences, seek advice, and contribute to discussions.

Plan:

Allocate regular time to participate, sharing insights and learning from others' experiences. Build virtual connections that foster support and collaboration.

5. Establishing a Supportive Environment with Family and Friends

Action Steps:

Share your financial goals with close family and friends. Encourage open discussions about financial matters.

Plan:

Create a supportive environment where ideas and challenges can be openly discussed. Involve loved ones in celebrating milestones, fostering a sense of shared accomplishment.

Nurturing a supportive network involves actively seeking mentorship, considering financial advisory services, forming peer accountability partnerships, engaging in online communities, and involving family and friends in your financial journey. By fostering meaningful connections, individuals can tap into a wealth of perspectives, experiences, and encouragement to navigate challenges and achieve long-term financial success.

Chapter 9: Conclusion

In conclusion, my exploration of the Nine-Figure Mindset has delved into foundational principles crucial for achieving extraordinary financial success. From fostering a growth mindset and setting clear goals to embracing innovation and building a supportive network, these principles serve as the pillars of financial accomplishment.

To recap, I underscored the importance of:

- **Cultivating a Growth Mindset:** Nurturing a mindset that welcomes challenges, views failures as learning opportunities, and consistently seeks self-improvement.

- **Precise Goal Setting:** Defining well-articulated, attainable goals and creating actionable plans to reach them.

- **Fostering Innovation:** Continually seeking innovative solutions, embracing change, and thinking beyond conventional boundaries.

- **Building a Supportive Network:** Surrounding oneself with mentors, peers, and loved ones who provide guidance, encouragement, and accountability.

To my readers, you now hold a comprehensive guide enriched with insights, exercises, and actionable strategies. It's not just a roadmap; it's an invitation to take charge. Your journey toward financial abundance is uniquely yours—embrace challenges as opportunities, celebrate victories, and consistently refine your path.

You possess the ability to redefine what's achievable. Your potential is not restricted by present circumstances; it's shaped by the choices you make and the actions you take. Seize the potential for growth, and let the Nine-Figure Mindset be a catalyst for transformation.

Bear in mind that this guide extends beyond monetary figures; it encapsulates a holistic approach to wealth, encompassing mindset, strategy, and impact. It's about creating a life of abundance, influence, and purpose.

In adopting the Nine-Figure Mindset, envision a future where your financial success aligns with your personal values, contributes to societal well-being, and leaves a lasting legacy. May this mindset serve as a guiding force, propelling you towards unprecedented achievements, both in your financial pursuits and personal fulfilment.

The journey doesn't culminate here; it evolves into a legacy. The principles you've embraced, the actions you've taken, and the growth you've experienced become part of a narrative that extends beyond individual success—a narrative that shapes the future landscape of financial possibilities.

Embark on this journey with resilience, creativity, and an unwavering commitment to your vision. The Nine-Figure Mindset isn't a destination; it's an ongoing evolution—a mindset propelling you to new heights, challenging the norm, and leaving an indelible mark on the world.

www.ingramcontent.com/pod-product-compliance
Lightning Source LLC
Chambersburg PA
CBHW072254310526
45795CB00012B/1265